Books in the Wildlife of the World series:

Wildlife of the World - China
Wildlife of the World - Costa Rica
Wildlife of the World - Madagascar
Wildlife of the World - South Africa

Coming soon:
Wildlife of the World - Japan

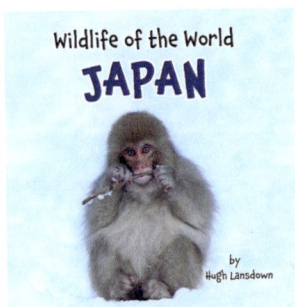

Visit *www.wildlifeoftheworld.com* to find out more about the books in the Wildlife of the World series.

Wildlife of the World

China

by

Hugh Lansdown

Text copyright © Hugh Lansdown 2025
Photography copyright © Hugh Lansdown 2025
All rights reserved.
ISBN: 978-1-917175-10-4

Hugh Lansdown has asserted his right under the Copyright, Designs and Patent Act 1988 to be identified as the author of this work.

This book is meant to be educational, informative and entertaining. Although the author and publisher have made every effort to ensure that the information in this book was correct at the time of publication, the author and publisher do not assume and hereby disclaim any liability to any party for loss, damage or disruption caused by errors or omissions, whether such errors or omissions result from negligence, accident or any other cause.

The names given to animals in the book and associated online media are the most appropriate English names the author was able to find based on visible characteristics. They don't represent a precise scientific identification, which in many cases would require the animal to be captured and a detailed examination carried out.

SECOND EDITION published 2025
by Natural Planet Books
Unit 134893
PO Box 7169
Poole
BH15 9EL

www.naturalplanetbooks.com

Library Cataloguing in Publication Data. A catalogue record for this book is available from the British Library.

All rights reserved. No part of this book may be reprinted or reproduced or utilised in any form or by electronic, mechanical or any other means, now known or hereafter invented, including photocopying or recording, or in any information storage or retrieval system, without the permission in writing from the publisher.

To Mum

...for your infinite support!

How to use this book

This is an 'Interactive' book, which means that as well as paper pages, it has digital ones containing videos, sound and slideshows.

How do I access the digital pages?

1 By scanning the QR codes

Throughout the book you will see Interactive Zones which look like this:

Just scan the black and white QR codes using a mobile phone, tablet or any device with a camera that can read QR codes.

2 By searching the Internet

If your device doesn't have a camera or can't read QR codes, you can just search the Internet for:

- **Hugh Lansdown photography**
- then click on **Books**
- **Wildlife of the World - China**
- **Media Links**

You'll see a list of all the digital pages with the page number in this book that each one is linked to.

Wildlife Extras!

Some wildlife pages in this book have hidden animals that haven't been labelled. See how many you can spot then check the list on page 48 to see if you got them all!

Contents

	Page
How to use this book	6
Contents	7
Map of China	8
Where is China?	9
Life in the Cities	11
The Central Mountains	15
The Northern Deserts	19
The Southern Forests	23
The Northern Hills	27
The Tibetan Plateau	31
The Great Wall of China	35
Pandas	38
Snub-nosed Monkeys	40
Conserving China's Wildlife	42
Answers	44
Index	46
Wildlife Extras	48

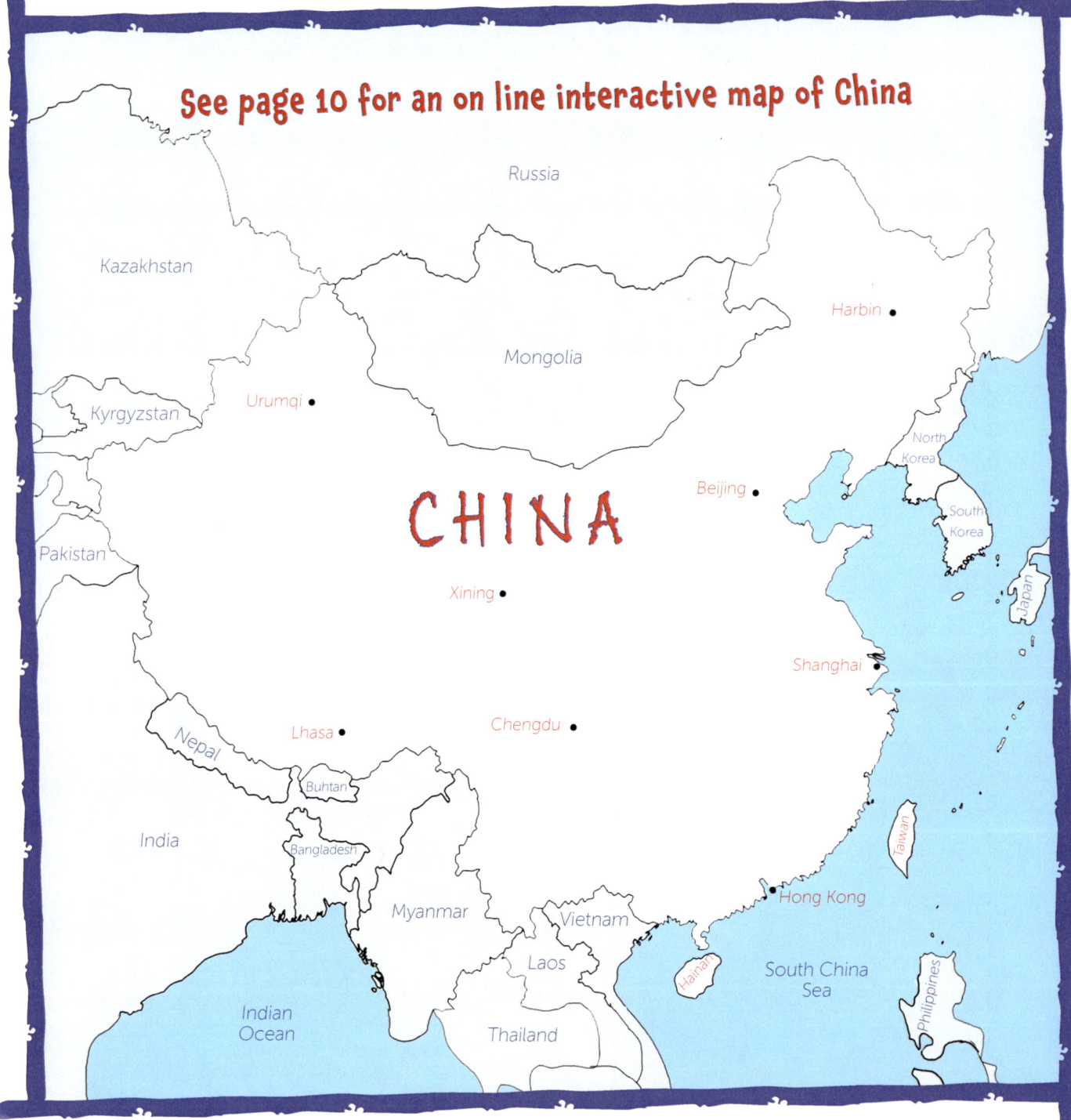

Where is China?

China is in Asia. It's the world's third biggest country and has the largest population... a whopping 1.4 billion people!

The huge size means that different regions have very different habitats. There are the world's highest mountains in the west, freezing deserts to the north and warm tropical forests in the south.

These habitats provide a home for all sorts of different animals and many live nowhere else in the world.

Read on to learn more about them!

It's over here... in Asia!

Interactive Map of China

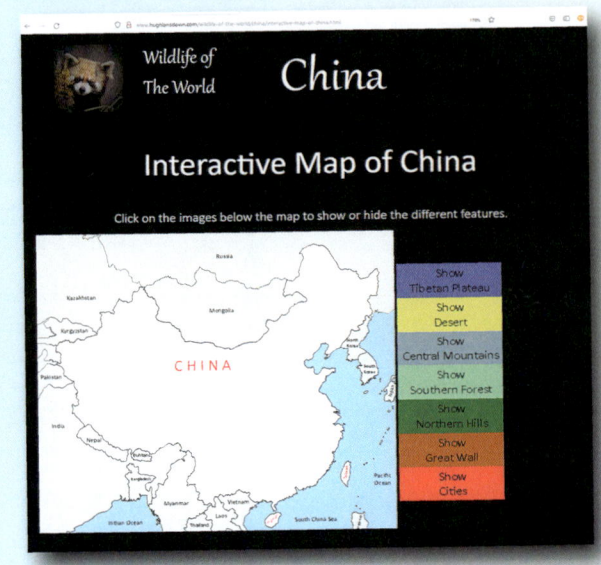

Modern China has developed from an ancient civilisation that goes back thousands of years. Traditionally, most of the people lived in lowlands in the south and east of the country.

INTERACTIVE ZONE!

Scan the QR code to explore the interactive map

(If you're not sure how, check page 6 for details.)

In recent years lots of people have been leaving the farmland and moving to work in the cities, which are rapidly growing in size. Today, six of the world's ten largest cities can be found in China.

Try loading the **Interactive Map** and clicking the buttons to show different regions such as deserts, forests and mountains.

You can also see the location of some major cities as well as the route of the Great Wall of China!

Life in the Cities

A surprising amount of wildlife can be found in China's cities. Some animals like **sparrows** and cockroaches do well because they eat the food that people waste, and birds like **grey herons** prey on fish living in the city lakes.

But when cities are built, valuable wildlife habitats are often destroyed… and some of the animals that used to live there are left homeless in the new concrete jungles.

Grey Heron

These birds are Lapwings, searching for a new home because the wetlands where they used to breed have been built on

WHAT LIVES IN THE CITIES?

Crested Myna

Praying Mantis

There are all sorts of fascinating animals that do manage to survive in China's cities.

Ponds in parks and gardens are home to many different types of frogs and fish while trees and bushes are perfect for insects like the **praying mantis** to creep about in, stalking their prey.

Crested mynas and other hungry birds search the plants for insects in the warm summer months and then feast on berries when autumn comes.

Tree Sparrows picking rice off a city street

Animals in cities usually depend on people to survive. Some eat the food we waste or live in our parks and gardens but others need an extra helping hand.

The **crested ibis** is a very rare bird that nearly became extinct, so when a city was being built in their Yangxian home, special areas were created just for the ibis. Now their numbers are increasing and they are even starting to spread to new areas nearby.

Humans aren't friends to **black-spotted frogs** though. They are a delicacy, so some people collect them from city ponds to make into a tasty meal!

HOW DO THEY SURVIVE THERE?

Black-spotted Frog

Crested Ibis

China's City Parks

Black-throated Tit

The building of huge modern cities can be a challenge for wildlife. But Chinese cities always include lots of parks full of trees and flowers, which provide a great home for insects and birds.

Sharp-eyed **black-throated tits** like to eat moths that live in the parks, but the **corymica moth** has a clever disguise. Its wings are full of holes so it looks like a rotten leaf and the birds leave it alone!

Visit the Interactive Zone to see more animals in China's city parks or check out the **Interactive Map** on page 10 for the location of some of the major cities.

Corymica Moth

INTERACTIVE ZONE!

Scan the QR code to see more wildlife from China's city parks

(If you're not sure how, check page 6 for details.)

The Central Mountains

Wild mountains with deep, forested valleys make up much of central China. The highest peaks have snow all year round, and some strange animals live there like **pandas** (page 38) and **golden takin**.

Takin are huge scary goats that sometimes attack people if they come too close!

Bamboo is common in the mountains and provides food for pandas as well as the beautiful **bamboo partridge**, a shy relative of the domestic chicken.

Golden Takin

Bamboo Partridge

WHAT LIVES IN THE MOUNTAINS?

It's difficult to travel or grow crops in the mountains, so very few people live there, which makes them a great place for all sorts of wildlife.

Masked palm civets are small carnivores that wander the forest at night and squirt a smelly spray out of their bottoms whenever they feel threatened!

Tibetan macaques are very large monkeys that only live in China. They feed on seeds and insects in the mountain forests but also like to steal food from humans if they can.

There are lots of different birds living in the mountains. The beautiful **red-billed leiothrix** likes to pick insects from trees on the mountain slopes, while black and white **forktails** search for them amongst rocks in the bottom of the valleys.

Masked Palm Civet

White-crowned Forktail

HOW DO THEY LIVE THERE?

Red-billed Leiothrix

The **doris map** is a beautiful butterfly that feeds on mountain flowers. They are endemic to the central Chinese mountains, which means it's the only place in the world they are found.

Doris Map butterfly

Mother and baby Tibetan Macaques

Feeding in the Mountains

It can be difficult to find enough to eat in the mountains, especially in harsh winter weather. But the beautiful **mountain bulbul** and agile **Chinese rock squirrel** are specially adapted to finding food on the steep, rocky mountain slopes.

Visit the Interactive Zone to watch some mountain animals feeding, or try the **Interactive Map** on page 10 to see where the central mountains are located.

Mountain Bulbul

INTERACTIVE ZONE!

Scan the QR code to see more mountain wildlife

(If you're not sure how, check page 6 for details.)

Chinese Rock Squirrel

The Northern Deserts

Large parts of northern China are covered in desert, where it's freezing cold at night but seriously hot in the daytime, and hardly ever rains. Because of this, not many plants can grow, so there isn't a lot for animals to eat.

The desert is not an easy place to survive... so the birds that live there, like **hoopoes** and **golden eagles,** have to roam over huge distances to find food.

Golden Eagle

Hoopoe in the Kubuqi Desert

WHAT LIVES IN THE DESERTS?

Because of the lack of water and plants in the desert, only animals that are specially adapted to life in these harsh, dry conditions can survive there.

Strange-looking **toadhead agama** lizards have developed thick eyelids to keep the sand out of their eyes and stand on tip-toe so their bodies don't get burnt by the hot sand.

Birds like **kestrels** and **crested larks** fly and find somewhere shady to rest during the hottest part of the day. They mainly hunt for insects like **dune beetles** to eat when it's cooler in the early morning and late evening.

Kestrel

Toadhead Agama Lizard

WHAT ARE DUNE BEETLES?

Dune beetles are little black beetles that have evolved for life in the desert sand dunes.

In the daytime they run very fast over the hot sand to stop their feet burning, only stopping to feed on scraps of dead plants or animals.

When they are mating, the female continues to roam the dunes, dragging the male with her!

Crested Lark eating a Dune Beetle

Dune Beetles mating, with the female dragging the male behind her!

INTERACTIVE ZONE!

Scan the QR code to watch a dune beetle hiding from danger

(If you're not sure how, check page 6 for details.)

Visit the Interactive Zone to watch a beetle burying itself in the sand, or try the **Interactive Map** on page 10 to see where the northern deserts are located.

Dune Beetle Escape

Dune beetles spend their time running across the desert in search of scraps of food to eat. They are one of the few insects that live there, so many types of predator like to eat them, including kestrels, larks and lizards.

To survive, the beetles have to stay alert, so as soon as they spot a predator they immediately stop running and quickly bury themselves in the sand to escape!

Dune Beetle feeding

The Southern Forests

In the far south near the equator, lie China's tropical southern forests... lush, humid rainforests that are home to a huge variety of different animals.

Finding a mate can be difficult in the dense forest, especially for animals like **oriental garden lizards** which are camouflaged a dull brown colour to stay hidden from predators.

But males have a clever trick for when they want to get themselves noticed. If a female or a rival male turns up, they start to display, and in less than a minute their head has turned bright red!

Male Oriental Garden Lizard

... displaying

... normal colour

WHAT LIVES IN THE RAINFOREST?

Many different types of animal live in China's lush, tropical rainforest and they have all sorts of ways of avoiding danger.

Chinese flying frogs have developed large, webbed feet which they use like four little parachutes, so they can leap out of trees and 'fly' away to escape from predators.

Like most birds, **light-vented bulbuls** have very sharp eyesight, so they can spot danger and quickly fly away.

Slugmoth caterpillars have sharp spines so birds like bulbuls don't want to eat them, and huge female **giant orb-weaver spiders** are just too big for the bulbuls to eat!

Chinese Flying Frog

Slugmoth Caterpillar

Can you spot the ten animals shown on these two pages, and guess how they all stay safe? (*Answers on page 44*).

HOW DO THEY SURVIVE THERE?

Light-vented Bulbul

Giant Orb-weaver Spider

Cicada

Rainforest Singer

Butterflies like the **red helen** use bright colours to attract a mate in the dense forest, but male **cicadas** have a different method… they 'sing' to the females. Their song is one of the loudest produced by any insect and can even permanently damage people's hearing if they get too close!

Visit the Interactive Zone to hear a male cicada singing in the Fujian southern forest, or the **Interactive Map** on page 10 to see where the southern forests are located.

INTERACTIVE ZONE!

Scan the QR code to hear a cicada singing

(If you're not sure how, check page 6 for details.)

Red Helen Butterfly feeding in the rainforest

The Northern Hills

The north-east of China is hilly and mostly covered in forest.

Summer is hot, dry and buzzing with invertebrates like the enormous **giant millipedes** which can grow up to 30cm long.

But in the bitterly cold winter months, trees lose their leaves and insects lie dormant. Only a few mammals and birds like the **Godlewski's bunting** stay active, hunting for food in the snow.

Godlewski's Bunting in winter

Giant Millipede in summer

WHAT LIVES IN THE HILLS?

Wildlife in the hills varies with the seasons, but **azure-winged magpies** roam them all year long in small, noisy flocks. In the warm summer months they feed on insects, eggs and small animals but switch to berries and seeds when the weather gets colder.

Butterflies like the beautiful **dragon swallowtail** drink nectar from summer flowers that grow in the hills. The freezing winter temperatures are much too cold for them to survive, but their pupae lie hidden, and when the weather starts to warm up in spring, a new generation of butterflies appears.

In summer **araneid spiders** catch small flying insects in their webs, but when the weather starts to get cold they die, leaving their eggs hidden beneath the snow. In spring when the snow thaws, tiny spiders hatch from the eggs and immediately start to spin new webs.

Azure-winged Magpie

Dragon Swallowtail

Araneid Spider

HOW DO THEY SURVIVE THERE?

Asiatic toads feed on insects and spiders, but when it gets cold in the autumn there isn't much food about, so they find a nice safe hole, climb in and sleep right through until spring!

Their skin has poison in, that stops predators like foxes trying to eat them. Sometimes in traditional Chinese medicine people squeeze the poison out of the toads and use it to treat diseases such as cancer.

Asiatic Toad

Northern Insects

Despite the freezing winter weather, a surprising variety of insects can be found in the northern hills.

The **spotted lanternfly** is a type of bug that feeds on trees by poking a sharp tube into their bark and then sucking up the sap inside. **Red and bronze ground beetles** are aggressive carnivores that use their long legs to chase and catch smaller insects to eat.

Visit the Interactive Zone for more insects from the northern hills, or the **Interactive Map** on page 10 to see where the northern hills are located.

Spotted Lanternfly

Red And Bronze Ground Beetle

INTERACTIVE ZONE!

Scan the QR code for more insects from the northern hills

(If you're not sure how, check page 6 for details.)

The Tibetan Plateau

The Tibetan Plateau is the world's biggest and highest plateau. It is also very remote... which makes it a great place for wildlife to live without being disturbed by people.

The most common mammal is the tiny **plateau pika,** which is a herbivore a bit like a cross between a mouse and a rabbit. Huge numbers of them live on the plateau, sometimes as many as twenty thousand in a single square kilometre!

Plateau Pika

Herd of Kiang

WHAT LIVES ON THE PLATEAU?

Many large herbivores live on the plateau including Tibetan antelope, gazelle and a type of wild horse called **kiang**. They are all specially adapted to survive the low oxygen levels at such high altitude.

There are also many carnivores, including **Tibetan foxes** on the grassland, **Pallas's cats** on rocky hillsides and **saker falcons** patrolling the skies.

Despite the cold temperatures, **Tibetan spring snakes** can also be found hidden under rocks. They live at the highest altitude of any snake in the world, using the heat from hot springs to stay warm.

Tibetan Fox

Pallas' Cat

Tibetan Spring Snake

Herbivores feed on the short grass and plants that grow right across the plateau. Carnivores, of course, eat the herbivores!

The foxes and cats mainly catch pika while packs of wolves hunt the Kiang and other large herbivores. **Lammergeier** feed on the bones of dead animals, dropping them from a great height to smash them open.

Saker falcons are fierce hunters that catch and eat small birds, but the males also fight each other for the best territories... like the two below.

WHAT FOOD DO THEY EAT?

Lammergeier carrying a wild sheep bone

Male Saker Falcons fighting

Vultures and Wolves

Wolves are some of the Tibetan Plateau's fiercest hunters. They roam the region in packs and when they make a kill, flocks of **vultures** arrive to pick over the remains. Sometimes cheeky vultures will even try to pinch some meat while the wolves are still feeding.

Visit the Interactive Zone to watch a wolf chasing vultures away from its kill, or try the **Interactive Map** on page 10 to see where the Tibetan Plateau is located.

Himalayan Griffon Vulture

INTERACTIVE ZONE!

Scan the QR code to see a wolf attacking vultures

(If you're not sure how, check page 6 for details.)

A pack of Wolves patrolling the plateau

The Great Wall

The **Great Wall of China** is an incredible line of ancient stone barriers across northern China which is over twenty thousand kilometres long!

The building work was started over two thousand years ago to keep invaders from the north out and help control trade. Today it's a popular attraction for thousands of tourists each year.

Much of the wall is overgrown with trees and plants, which makes it a great place for insects like the strange-looking **longhorn beetle** below, with its huge antennae.

An overgrown section of the Great Wall

Longhorn Beetle

WHAT LIVES ON THE WALL?

All sorts of different wildlife lives on the overgrown sections of wall. **Longhorn beetles** eat the leaves of some of the plants that grow there, and butterflies like the **white-letter hairstreak** feed on nectar from the flowers.

These insects then attract a variety of predators. **Scutigerid centipedes** use their many long legs to chase small insects and pounce on them, while **praying mantises** stealthily stalk their prey across the stones.

Ordos racerunner lizards lie hidden in cracks between the stones, waiting to ambush an unsuspecting insect. After a meal they like to sunbathe on the warm stones to digest it... keeping a wary eye out for falcons.

Scutigerid Centipede

Ordos Racerunner Lizard

Amur Falcon

WHY DO THEY LIVE THERE?

Amur falcons usually catch insects like beetles and bees in flight but will also land and pick them off the wall... as well as the occasional lizard!

The wall makes a good home because the stones get warm in the sunshine and the many cracks and crevices provide safe places for small animals to hide in.

White-letter Hairstreak

Praying Mantis

Giant Panda in the Bifengxia breeding centre

Pandas

The most famous Chinese animals are probably the pandas. There are two different types, but they aren't actually very closely related.

The **giant panda** is a large black and white bear which is popular in children's stories and famous throughout the world but only found in China.

The **red panda** is a small, very cute relative of weasels and otters that lives in China but is also found in the nearby countries of India and Bhutan.

Although not closely related, the two types of panda have quite a lot in common. They both feed mainly on bamboo but can also eat fruit, eggs and even small animals. They are also both endangered and rarely seen in the wild.

A pair of wild Red Pandas

The Chinese authorities have made big efforts to save giant pandas from extinction by breeding them in special centres and then releasing some back into their original wild habitat. This seems to be working and the wild population is slowly starting to increase.

Visit the Interactive Zone to see videos of both red and giant pandas feeding.

INTERACTIVE ZONE!

Scan the QR code to watch pandas feeding

(If you're not sure how, check page 6 for details.)

Snub-nosed Monkeys

Baby Golden Snub-nosed Monkey

Snub-nosed monkeys are a very rare and rather unusual group of primates, most of which only live in China.

They are found in remote forests high up in the mountains, so they are difficult to study, and not much is known about them.

There are five different species, two of which are shown here. **Yunnan snub-nosed monkeys** are black and white with very thick, shaggy fur. They need it to keep warm because they live at an altitude of over 4000 meters... the highest of any monkey in the world.

Golden snub-nosed monkeys are also very shaggy and look even stranger. Babies are a cream colour, but adults have bright orange fur with pale blue faces.

Adult male Yunnan Snub-nosed Monkey

Adult male Golden Snub-nosed Monkey

They live in large, noisy troops and roam the mountain forests in search of their favourite food, lichens. If two troops meet there is often a fierce battle with males attacking each other while the females guard their young.

Visit the Interactive Zone to see more snub-nosed monkeys, hear their strange calls and learn about how they behave.

INTERACTIVE ZONE!

Scan the QR code to see more snub-nosed monkeys

(If you're not sure how, check page 6 for details.)

WHAT ARE THE PROBLEMS?

Conserving China's Wildlife

Dead badgers and cats in a Chinese market

As in most countries in the world, the wildlife of China is under threat in various different ways.

Traditionally, some Chinese people have eaten wild animals and caught birds to put in cages, and this is becoming a problem as the human population increases.

Traditional Chinese medicines are sometimes made from parts of wild animals such as pangolin scales, rhino horn and tiger bones.

As Chinese people become richer, they are prepared to pay large amounts of money for these medicines, which encourages poachers to kill the animals.

Chinese photographers waiting for Red-billed Magpies

CAN THEY BE FIXED?

Caged Red-billed Starlings in a Chinese market

Poaching is a major reason some animals are in danger of disappearing. There are signs things are starting to improve though, with Chinese influencers campaigning for protection of endangered animals, and the government banning the sale of wild meat.

Birdwatching is also becoming popular, including photographing birds instead of catching them to eat or put in cages.

Let's hope everyone will work together and make sure China's amazing wildlife continues to survive into the future.

Red-billed Magpies eating food put out by bird photographers

Rhino horns for sale in a Beijing shop

Answers

to the animals on pages 24 and 25 and how they stay safe.

1 Buff-tip Moth

Buff-tip moths are camouflaged like broken twigs, and sit very still hoping predators won't notice them.

2 Chinese Flying Frog

Chinese flying frogs 'fly' away from danger, gliding on their huge feet!

3 Narcissus Flycatcher

Males narcissus flycatchers are brightly coloured to attract females. They spot predators using their sharp eyesight, then quickly fly away to safety.

4 Stick Insect

Stick insects look like little twigs, so like the buff-tips, they keep very still if there's danger around.

5 Slugmoth Caterpillar

Slugmoth caterpillars use their sharp spines for protection.

WHAT LIVES IN THE RAINFOREST?

Many different types of animal live in China's lush, tropical rainforest and they have all sorts of ways of avoiding danger.

Chinese flying frogs have developed large webbed feet which they use like four little parachutes so they can leap out of trees and 'fly' away to escape from predators.

Like most birds, **light-vented bulbuls** have very sharp eyesight, so they can spot danger and quickly fly away.

Slugmoth caterpillars have sharp spines so birds like bulbuls don't want to eat them, and huge female **giant orb-weaver spiders** are just too big for the bulbuls to eat!

Chinese Flying Frog

Slugmoth Caterpillar

Can you spot the ten animals shown on these two pages, and guess how they stay safe? (Answers on page 44).

HOW DO THEY SURVIVE THERE?

Light-vented Bulbul

Giant Orb-weaver Spider

10 Light-vented Bulbul

Like the flycatcher, bulbuls rely on their sharp eyesight to spot predators and fly to safety.

9 Atractomorpha Grasshopper

These grasshoppers are camouflaged like the grass they live in and are very difficult for predators to spot. They also use their powerful hind legs to leap to safety if they're threatened.

Grasshopper revealed

6 Assassin Bug

This assassin bug's green colour helps hide it from birds, but also allows it to sneak up on its prey without being seen.

7 Male giant orb weaver

Male orb weavers aren't giant at all! Their tiny size saves them from hungry females because they're too small to be worth eating!

8 Female giant orb weaver

The female's huge size means she's too big for most birds to eat... and in fact small birds occasionally get caught in her web, and she eats them!

Index

Amur falcon 37
Araneid Spider 28–29
Asiatic Toad 29
Assassin Bug 25, 45
Azure-winged Magpie 28
Bamboo Partridge 15
Beetle 15, 20, 21, 22, 30, 35, 36, 48
Beet Webworm Moth 28, 48
Black-spotted Frog 13
Black-throated Tit 14
Buff-tip Moth 24, 44
Butterfly 17, 26, 28, 32, 36, 37, 48
Chinese Flying Frog 24, 44
Chinese Goral 16, 48
Chinese Rock Squirrel 18
Chough 17, 48
Chukar Partridge 35, 48
Cicada 26
Corymica Moth 14
Crested Ibis 13
Crested Lark 20, 21

Crested Myna 12
Doris Map Butterfly 17
Dragon Swallowtail 28
Dune Beetle 20, 21, 22
Feral Pigeon 12, 48
Frogs and Toads 13, 24, 29, 44
Golden Takin 15
Great Wall of China 7, 35–37
Garden Fence Lizard 23
Giant Millipede 27
Giant Orb-weaver Spider 24, 25, 45
Giant Panda 38–39
Godlewski's Bunting 27
Golden Eagle 19
Grasshopper 25, 45
Grey Heron 9, 11, 48
Ground Beetle 30
Himalayan Griffon Vulture 34, 48
Hoopoe 19
Horned Lark 20, 48
Kestrel 20

Kiang 31, 32, 33, 52
Lammergeier 33
Lapwing 11
Light-vented Bulbul 24–25, 45
Little Egret 9, 48
Lizard 20, 23, 36
Longhorn Beetle 35, 36
Lycaenid Butterfly 32, 48
Map of China 8
Masked Palm Civet 16
Moth 14, 24, 28, 44, 48
Mountain Bulbul 18
Narcissus Flycatcher 24, 44
Oil Beetle 15, 48
Ordos Racerunner Lizard 36
Oriental Garden Lizard 23
Pallas' Cat 32
Plateau Pika 31, 33, 48
Praying Mantis 12, 37
QR Codes 6, 48
Red-billed Leiothrix 16, 17
Red-billed Magpie 43
Red-billed Starling 43

Red Fox 29, 48
Red Helen Butterfly 26
Red Panda 38–39
Red-rumped Swallow 13, 48
Saker Falcon 32, 33
Scutigerid Centipede 36
Slugmoth Caterpillar 24, 44
Snub-nosed Monkey 1, 40–41
Spider 25, 28, 29, 45
Spotted Lanternfly 30
Stick Insect 24, 44
Tibetan Antelope 32, 48
Tibetan Fox 32
Tibetan Gazelle 33, 48
Tibetan Macaques 16–17
Tibetan Spring Snake 32
Toadhed Agama 20
Tree Sparrow 12
Uplands Buzzard 32, 48
Wallcreeper 17, 48
White-crowned Forktail 16
White-letter Hairstreak 36, 37
Wolf 33, 34

Wildlife Extras!

On some pages, there are photos of animals that haven't been labelled, usually in the background or hidden in vegetation.

See how many you can spot, then check the list below to see if you got them all. You can also scan the QR code above to find out more about them.

Page	Animals
9	Two little egrets and a grey heron at the edge of the lake on the left.
12	A flock of feral pigeons flying behind the praying mantis.
13	Three red-rumped swallows flying behind the crested ibis.
15	An oil beetle on a grass stalk in front of the bamboo partridge.
16	Two Chinese gorals on the cliff behind the palm civet.
17	Three choughs flying and a wallcreeper on the cliff behind the monkeys.
20	Two horned larks behind the toadhead agama lizard.
24, 25	See pages 44 and 45 for details.
28	A beet webworm moth hiding amongst the leaves below the magpie.
29	A red fox on the cliff behind the toad.
32	Five Tibetan antelopes on the plateau behind the Pallas's cat, a lycaenid butterfly to the left of the Tibetan fox and an upland buzzard above it.
33	A plateau pika at the front near the fighting falcons, and three Tibetan gazelle on the plateau behind it.
34	Two Himalayan griffon vultures circling above the hills in the top left.
35	Two chukar partridges on the steps of the overgrown wall.

Acknowledgements

Many people have helped me in writing this book, and I would like to thank some of them here:

Tina Ji and Maggie Zhao of Harrow Beijing for getting me through the daily challenges of life in China.

Terry Townsend of Birding Beijing for advice on photographing wildlife in China, conservation issues and the suitability of the text.

Adam Hathaway for graphic design and layout advice.

Lydia Wang for advice on the suitability of the text.

Geraint 'Sid' Francis and ZZ for arranging and leading trips to remote regions of China.

Barbara 'Bob' Justham for getting me to Yunnan province and into the northern desert.

Beth, Cat, Alice and Ellie at Rowanvale for their invaluable advice, support and patience.

All photos, video clips and sound recordings of wildlife in this book and on the associated web pages were taken by Hugh Lansdown in China.

All the animals photographed were wild and free except for the giant panda at the Bifengxia Panda Research Centre on page 38 and the caged red-billed starlings on page 43.

About the Author

Hugh Lansdown is a Welsh wildlife photographer who has travelled extensively, and his images have appeared in hundreds of books, magazines and other publications across the globe.

He is also heavily involved in conservation at home in Wales, working for local wildlife charities, carrying out habitat management work and giving talks about wildlife conservation.

You can find out more about Hugh's photography, writing and conservation work by visiting his website or signing up to his monthly newsletters:

www.hughlansdown.com/newsletters.html

Sneaky Animals!

A few random animals seem to have sneaked into the book when Hugh wasn't looking...

Page 2   - a stick insect

Page 3   - two young golden snub-nosed monkeys

Page 5   - an Asian barred owlet

Page 6   - a Dora's Harlequin butterfly and a bush cricket

Page 7   - a crested ibis

Page 46 - a great-spotted woodpecker

Page 51 - a Chinese flying frog

What did you think of Wildlife of the World - China?

A big thank you for buying this book. It means a lot that you chose this book specifically from such a wide range on offer.

We do hope you enjoyed it.

Book reviews are incredibly important for an author. All feedback helps them improve their writing for future projects and for developing this edition. If you are able to spare a few minutes to post a review on Amazon or Goodreads, that would be much appreciated.

Kiang mare and foal on the Tibetan Plateau

www.ingramcontent.com/pod-product-compliance
Lightning Source LLC
Chambersburg PA
CBRC091204070526
44584CB00008B/334